POWER PLAY

The Spanish-American War

Kimberley Heuston

Steck Vaughn™

A Harcourt Achieve Imprint

www.Steck-Vaughn.com
1-800-531-5015

Power Play: The Spanish-American War
By Kimberley Heuston

Photo Acknowledgements
Cover ©The Art Archive/Library of Congress/Laurie Platt Winfrey; p. 5
©CORBIS; p. 6–7 ©Bettman/CORBIS; p. 9 ©The Granger Collection,
New York; p. 10–11 ©CORBIS; p. 13 l, r ©The Granger Collection, New
York; p. 17 ©The Granger Collection, New York; p. 18 ©The Granger
Collection, New York; p. 20–21 ©The Granger Collection, New York;
p. 23 ©The Granger Collection, New York; p. 25 ©The Granger
Collection, New York; p. 27 ©Bettman/CORBIS; p. 28 J.S. Pughe–
Courtesy of the Library of Congress.

Illustration Acknowledgements
Steve Stankiewicz p. 15.

ISBN-13: 978-1-4190-2310-1
ISBN-10:   1-4190-2310-1

© 2007 Harcourt Achieve Inc.

Printed in China

3 4 5 6 7 8 0940 15 14 13 12
4500369376

Table of Contents

War Next Door

The year was 1897. On the island just south of Florida, a war was underway. The Spanish had ruled the island of Cuba for 400 years. Now, Cubans wanted freedom.

The Cuban rebels fought a brutal war. They **ambushed** Spanish army units. They burned sugar **plantations**. They threatened Cubans who worked on foreign-owned farms.

The Spanish fought back. They sent 200,000 troops to the island. If Cuban farmers helped the rebels, the Spanish burned their fields. Spanish soldiers forced half a million Cubans into prison camps. Tens of thousands died.

U.S. newspapers reported it all. The New York *World* wrote, "Blood on the roadsides, blood in the fields, blood on the doorsteps, blood, blood, blood!"

Americans were horrified. Many of them didn't like having a Spanish colony near the U.S. border, anyway. Newspaper editorials urged the government to help the rebels. Yet, U.S. troops had never fought outside North America. Should they really try to push the Spanish out of the Caribbean? Was the United States ready for such a war?

President William McKinley did not want to go to war.
The events in Cuba made it hard for him to remain neutral.

Chapter One

Remember the *Maine!*

President William McKinley hated war. He had fought in the American Civil War thirty years earlier. Nearly 600,000 soldiers died in that conflict. McKinley didn't want to lose more young Americans. In March 1897, he gave his first speech as President. He said that Americans should never go to war "until every **agency** of peace has failed."

The war in Cuba tested the President's promise. McKinley tried to end the conflict peacefully. He **negotiated** with the Spanish. He urged Spain to

pull out of Cuba. He made some progress. Then riots broke out in the city of Havana. The violence threatened Americans who lived there.

At home, the cry for war grew louder. McKinley's critics said his **strategy** was weak. They nicknamed him "Wobbly Willie."

In January 1898, McKinley decided to act. He sent the USS *Maine* to Cuba. The warship was bigger than any ship in the Spanish navy. It had a crew of 374 men. It carried big guns. Thick armor guarded its sides. McKinley hoped the *Maine* would protect American citizens without starting a war.

The USS *Maine* floats in Havana Bay.

Mystery of the *Maine*

The *Maine* steamed into Havana Bay. She let down her anchor. Three weeks passed. There were no attacks on American property. McKinley's plan seemed to be working.

Then came the night of February 15, 1898. The *Maine* bobbed peacefully at anchor. At 9 P.M. a horn sounded. It was time to turn in for the night. Sailors went below to their beds. One by one, the ship's lights went out. Two officers stayed on deck. A warm breeze blew through the harbor. Everything was still.

Suddenly, a blast broke the silence. A second explosion rang out. It tossed the *Maine* part way out of the water. Pieces of the ship flew through the air. Cement rained down on the deck. Steel railings dropped from the sky. Lieutenant John Blandin saw the destruction. A piece of concrete hit his head, but he was not badly hurt. He and the other officer hurried to help their shipmates.

Four Spanish warships soon arrived. Blandin **boarded** one of them. The *Maine* burned furiously. In the firelight, they all searched for survivors.

Spanish doctors worked hard. They tried to save the American sailors. In the end, there were more bodies than survivors. Some 266 American sailors died in the explosion.

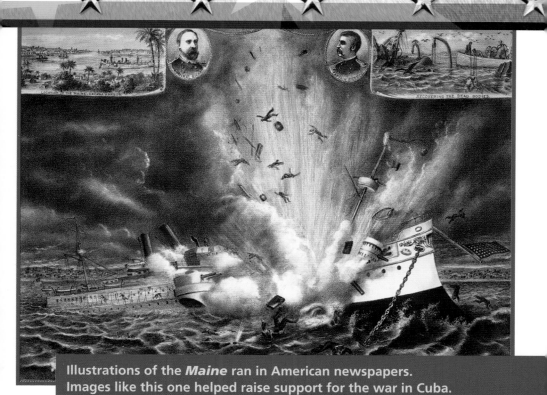

Illustrations of the *Maine* ran in American newspapers. Images like this one helped raise support for the war in Cuba.

Newspapers in the United States blamed the tragedy on the Spanish. The New York *Journal* ran a huge headline: "THE WARSHIP *MAINE* WAS SPLIT IN TWO BY AN ENEMY'S SECRET … MACHINE." The paper offered a $50,000 reward for information about the blast.

The U.S. government investigated. It found no evidence of a bomb or torpedo. It did find one possible cause. The *Maine*'s steam engine was powered by a coal-burning furnace. The ship's **ammunition** was stored near the furnace. Hot coals could have exploded and ignited the ammunition.

The Spanish denied responsibility. They had no reason to anger the United States. They didn't want American troops joining the war. Besides, they had helped to rescue the *Maine*'s crew.

By this time, though, it was too late.

Into the World

The United States had expanded quickly. In 1800, most Americans lived on the East Coast. To the west lay millions of acres of land. Native Americans claimed much of the territory. Yet, the new Americans were proud of their democracy. They believed in the idea of **Manifest Destiny**. They felt it was their duty to expand the nation from the Atlantic Ocean to the Pacific Ocean. So, they moved west.

By 1890, European settlers filled the continent. Native Americans had been forced onto reservations. The United States stretched from sea to sea.

Images like this one showing the wreck of the *Maine* forced McKinley into war.

Next, the nation expanded overseas. American companies bought land and businesses in other countries. By 1898, the United States had over $50 million **invested** in Cuba alone. Another $151 million went to Europe. About $200 million more went to Mexico. Meanwhile, the U.S. military reached into the Pacific Ocean. The Navy built bases in Samoa and Hawaii.

Until now, Americans had tried to stay out of European conflicts. Yet, Cuba lay just 144 km (90 miles) south of Florida. Cubans were crying out for help. The United States was supposed to stand for freedom. Should Americans watch and do nothing?

By April 1898, most people wanted the United States to support Cuba. Their slogan was, "Remember the *Maine*!"

On April 11, McKinley stopped wobbling. He sent a message to Congress. The United States must **liberate** Cuba from Spanish rule, it said. Spain and the United States were about to go to war.

Exciting! News! Exaggerated!

Joseph Pulitzer was born in Hungary. He came to the United States in 1864. He was only 17 years old. He had no money or friends, but this was America. Pulitzer could be anything he wanted to be. He decided to be a newspaperman. He worked hard. He saved money. In 1883, he bought a New York newspaper called the *World*.

Pulitzer chose a good time to run a newspaper. Paper was cheap. Public schools were free. More people could read than ever before.

There was another reason for Pulitzer's success. He created a new kind of newspaper called a **tabloid.** He printed big headlines. He ran lots of pictures. That made his newspaper fun to read. Pulitzer also sold lots of ads. He dropped the price of his paper. In 1896, the *World* cost just two cents. Nearly everyone could afford that.

Other newspapers began to copy Pulitzer's ideas. Soon, Pulitzer found himself in competition with William Randolph Hearst.

Hearst owned the *New York Journal*. He and Pulitzer hated each other. They stole each other's reporters. They stole each other's stories. Still, they agreed on one thing. War was good for business.

Both Hearst and Pulitzer sent writers, photographers, and illustrators to Cuba. They sent artists as well. These representatives sent back stories designed to shock Americans.

Hearst knew the power of images. One of his famous illustrators was Frederick Remington. Remington got bored. He wanted to return home. "Please remain," Hearst supposedly answered. "You supply the pictures and I'll supply the war."

Today, Pulitzer Prizes are given each year to promote excellence in writing and the arts. They were created by Pulitzer in his will. It's funny. Pulitzer never would have won his own prize!

This is what most newspapers looked like 100 years ago.

This is what Joseph Pulitzer's newspaper looked like.

Chapter Two

To War!

After the *Maine* sank, the U.S. Navy prepared for war. At the time, the Secretary of the Navy was sick. The assistant secretary took on the challenge. His name was Teddy Roosevelt. He would go on to become President of the United States.

Roosevelt was proud of the U.S. Navy. The United States owned some of the most advanced warships in the world. The navy could fight a war in any corner of the globe.

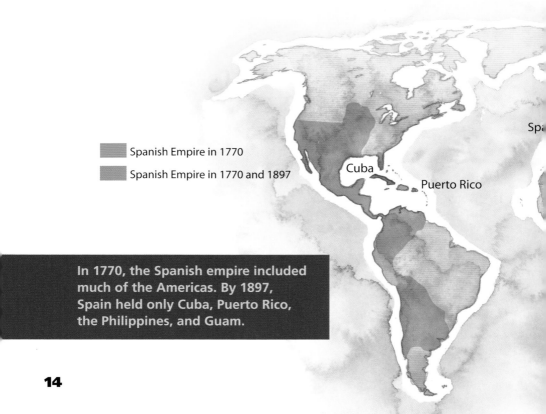

Spanish Empire in 1770

Spanish Empire in 1770 and 1897

Cuba

Puerto Rico

Sp

In 1770, the Spanish empire included much of the Americas. By 1897, Spain held only Cuba, Puerto Rico, the Philippines, and Guam.

Spain, however, was in **decline**. Once, Spain had the world's largest empire. By the 1500s, Spain controlled the Philippines. By 1770, they ruled much of North, Central, and South America.

In the early 1800s, Spain began to lose power. A **revolutionary** named Simón Bolívar rose up in Latin America. He **unified** several colonies in a revolt against Spain. Those colonies declared independence. The United States supported them. In 1823, President James Monroe issued his Monroe Doctrine. The Doctrine forbid European countries from creating any new colonies in the Americas.

By the 1890s, the Spanish empire had shrunk to four colonies. They were Cuba, Puerto Rico, the Philippines, and Guam.

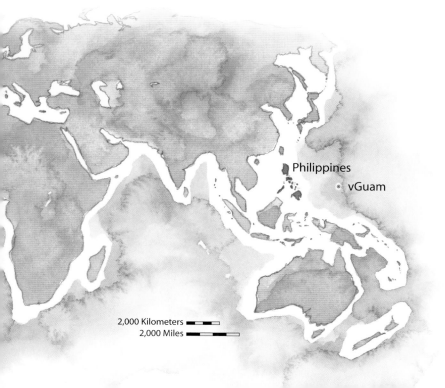

Philippines

vGuam

2,000 Kilometers
2,000 Miles

By 1898, the U.S. Navy was planning for war. Roosevelt contacted Commodore George Dewey, the head of America's Asian fleet. Roosevelt told Dewey to get ready. It was time to invade the Philippines. Spain had warships in the Philippines. If a war began, those ships would steam toward Cuba.

On April 25, 1898, the United States declared war on Spain. Dewey launched Roosevelt's plan. Before dawn on May 1, the U.S. Asian fleet sailed to the Philippines and into Manila Harbor. Spanish guns opened fire. Shells filled the air. Most of them fell harmlessly into the water.

Dewey decided not to waste ammunition. He waited. Soon the Spanish fleet was within range. Dewey gave his captain a simple order. "You may fire when you are ready, Gridley."

The sound of big guns split the air. Spanish warships began to splinter. Several caught fire. Flames leaped from the decks. The broken Spanish fleet littered the bay.

By noon the battle was over. It was a total victory for the United States. The Americans had sunk or captured every Spanish ship. Not a single American sailor died.

The Spanish lost ten warships at Manila Bay. American shells were deadly accurate.

A Rocky Start

After the victory at Manila Bay, Americans caught war fever. Young men rushed to join the U.S. Army. Within weeks, over 200,000 people signed up for duty. Even Teddy Roosevelt quit his navy job and joined the army. He formed a **brigade** of volunteers. Over 20,000 men applied for 1,000 places in his Rough Riders brigade.

U.S. troops set up camp near Daiquiri in Cuba in 1898.

The army was **overwhelmed** by the number of volunteers. The army ran out of uniforms and guns. So it used old Civil War supplies. The old rifles gave off clouds of smoke when they were fired. Soldiers wore clothes left over from the last war.

The first units left for Cuba. The navy didn't have enough boats. They rented boats from shipping companies. There still wasn't enough room. Some cavalry had to leave their horses at home.

The operation was a mess. Many soldiers were too excited to care. Ogden Wells fought with the Rough Riders. "It is very pleasant sailing through the tropic seas toward the unknown," wrote Wells. "The men on the ship are young and strong. We are eager to face what lies before us."

The first units arrived in Cuba on June 22, 1898. The beaches lay empty. The Spanish had pulled back to guard inland cities. The soldiers set up camp.

Army conditions had been bad in the states. They were even worse in Cuba. Supplies took forever to arrive. Food often spoiled during the trip. Gunpowder arrived wet and useless. The army didn't have enough tents. Some soldiers had to sleep in the mud. Lice infected their hair. Even cheerful Ogden Wells got discouraged. "In the open places," he wrote, "the sun was like a furnace and the packs were like lead."

Into Battle

In a week, the U.S. Army launched a **campaign** to take the Cuban city of Santiago. It was a difficult task. Santiago lay behind three hills. Spanish troops guarded the hills. Paths were steep and narrow through thick jungle. The Americans marched on. They sweated in their wool uniforms. They waded through ankle-deep mud.

The first hill was called El Caney. A tiny town sat at the top. Five hundred Spanish soldiers defended the town. On the first of July, over five thousand American troops started up the hill. They marched through tall grass. Rifles fired at them. Soldiers began to fall. The Spanish were outnumbered ten to one. Yet, they held off the Americans for ten hours.

Finally, the best American sharpshooters moved to the front. They began to pick off the enemy. By late afternoon, El Caney fell.

Meanwhile, thousands of American troops moved on Kettle Hill. The attack slowed under Spanish fire. Teddy Roosevelt got **impatient**. The Americans needed to make a bold move, he thought. Roosevelt pranced his horse up and down the line of troops. Finally, he ordered his men to charge.

Roosevelt rode with a pistol in one hand. He held a sword in the other. He led the Rough Riders up Kettle Hill. With them went the 10th Cavalry, an African-American **regiment**. They neared the top of the hill. Roosevelt saw the Spanish fleeing down the other side. The Americans now held Kettle Hill.

The Rough Riders turned next to San Juan Hill. They moved to reinforce the American 1st and 2nd Divisions. Together, the troops took the hill. The last of the Spanish forces retreated.

The Rough Riders pause at the top of Kettle Hill. Teddy is in the center, with the red shirt.

One last battle had to be fought. On the morning of July 3, the Spanish Caribbean fleet tried to flee Cuba. The U.S. Navy was waiting. One surprised American officer shouted, "Commodore, they are coming right at us!"

Commodore Schley was head of the American forces. He shouted back, "Well, go right at them!" By the end of the day, the Spanish fleet lay in ruins.

Two weeks later, the two sides declared a **truce**. The fighting in Cuba was over. The United States and Spain began negotiating a peace settlement.

The war in the Caribbean lasted less than a month. Cuba had fallen. American troops also had seized Puerto Rico easily. About 460 American soldiers died on both fronts.

The army had made a lot of mistakes. The war taught officers that they had to plan more carefully. Food, weapons, uniforms, and shelter weren't easy to supply. Illnesses had spread quickly among the troops. In the end, ten times more soldiers died from disease than from battle.

Still, the war brought the country together. It had been only 33 years since the American Civil War. Older people remembered it well. North and South had spent four years destroying each other. Hatreds from the conflict still **lingered**.

Now, many Americans were proud of their victory. The nation had come together. In Cuba, Southerners had fought alongside Northerners. Blacks had fought alongside whites. Lieutenant John J. Pershing commanded the African-American 10th Cavalry. He wrote that his soldiers had fought "shoulder to shoulder." They didn't think about "race or color." They cared only about "their common duty as Americans."

According to Secretary of State John Hay, it was "a splendid little war."

African Americans, who made up the 10th Cavalry, participated in the charge up San Juan Hill in Cuba.

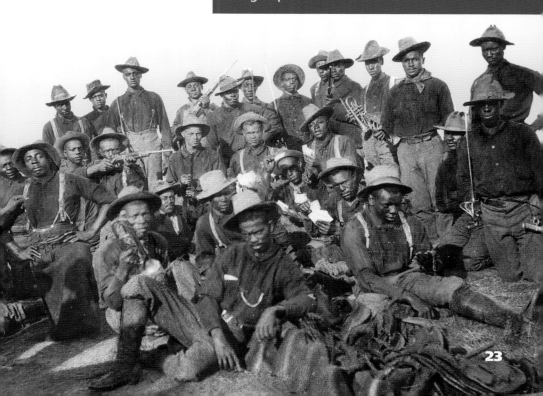

The Unlikely Hero

Theodore Roosevelt was an unlikely war hero. As a child, he was small and sickly. He had a high, scratchy voice. His eyes were weak. He had asthma. He often slept sitting up so that he could breathe.

Yet Roosevelt had a quick mind. He had **determination**. His father gave him some advice. "Without the help of the body, the mind cannot go as far as it should," he said. "You must *make* your body. It is hard ... but I know you will do it."

Roosevelt got to work. He lifted weights. He hiked mountains. He made his body strong.

Meanwhile, he rose quickly in politics. His family was wealthy. They knew important people in New York. By his mid-thirties, Roosevelt was New York City's police commissioner. At 39, he became Assistant Secretary of the U.S. Navy.

Then the Spanish-American War started. Roosevelt couldn't just watch. He **resigned** from his navy post to form the Rough Riders.

The Rough Riders were an odd group. Most of them were cowboys. Some were American Indians. Some were college boys from the Ivy League. Despite their name, they had few horses in Cuba, so they weren't really riders.

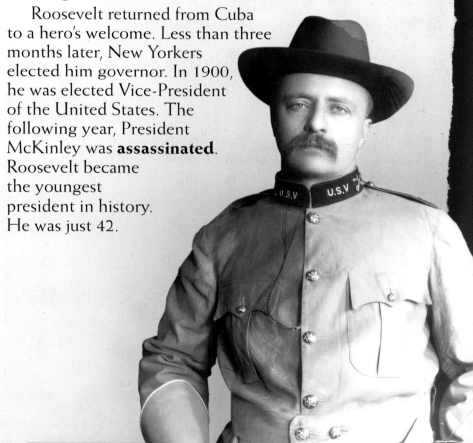

Roosevelt took good care of his men. He got them light-weight uniforms. He bought food for them with his own money. In Tampa, Florida, his men had to get to a ship. They had no transportation. Roosevelt stopped a coal train by standing in its tracks. He waved his men aboard.

Roosevelt returned from Cuba to a hero's welcome. Less than three months later, New Yorkers elected him governor. In 1900, he was elected Vice-President of the United States. The following year, President McKinley was **assassinated**. Roosevelt became the youngest president in history. He was just 42.

Teddy Roosevelt and his Rough Riders received the most publicity of any unit in the army. He went on to become the twenty-sixth President of the United States.

Chapter Three

A Splendid Little War?

After the surrender in Cuba, the United States and Spain began peace talks. Yet, there was unfinished business in the Philippines. Like the Cubans, Filipinos were rebelling against Spanish rule. In July, 20,000 American troops collected around Manila. They joined with 10,000 Filipino rebels. Spain was in no position to fight and quickly surrendered.

The victory was complete. Americans stood guard in the last four of Spain's former colonies: Cuba, the Philippines, Puerto Rico, and Guam.

Now, a great debate began. Americans had fought to free these people from Spanish rule. Would U.S. troops simply go home? Or would the Americans become colonial rulers themselves?

Filipino rebel leader Emilio Aguinaldo had fought the Spanish for years. He wanted the United States out. He wanted freedom for the Filipinos. Aguinaldo declared the Philippines independent.

Many Americans had other ideas for the Philippines. The Philippines would make a great shipping base for trade with Asia. Many business

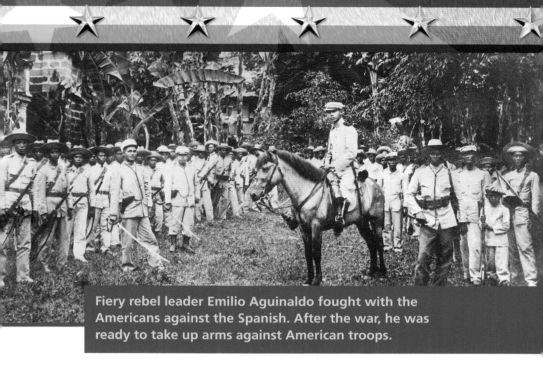

Fiery rebel leader Emilio Aguinaldo fought with the Americans against the Spanish. After the war, he was ready to take up arms against American troops.

leaders were in favor of this. If the United States left, they argued, another country would step in.

President McKinley wasn't comfortable taking over from the Spanish. Still, he eventually decided the Americans had to stay. The United States was wealthier than the Philippines, he argued. Americans were better educated. McKinley didn't think the Filipinos could govern themselves. Surely, Americans would help them by staying.

McKinley's position made some Americans furious. Critics of the war had already formed the Anti-Imperialist League. Its members included businessman Andrew Carnegie and writer Mark Twain. Ruling another country was un-American, they claimed. U.S. actions, they said, were a "war against liberty."

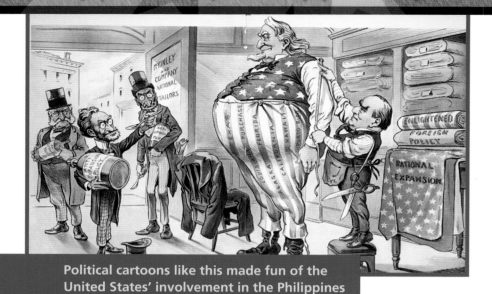

Political cartoons like this made fun of the United States' involvement in the Philippines and other former Spanish colonies.

In February 1899, the anti-imperialists lost the debate. Spain and the United States signed the Treaty of Paris. Guam and Puerto Rico became U.S. territories. They had their own governments. Yet, they were part of the United States.

In 1900, the Cubans wrote a constitution for their new country. At the time, U.S. troops were still on the island. American Secretary of War Elihu Root watched closely from Washington. He made a change to the Cuban constitution. It gave American troops the right to return. It also gave the United States a naval base on the island. Root wrote this so-called Platt Amendment himself.

The Cubans unhappily accepted the amendment. In 1902, most U.S. troops went home. The American naval base, however, still exists today. It is located at Guantánamo Bay.

The Philippines proved to be the toughest test. First, the United States bought the colony from Spain for $20 million. Soon, Aguinaldo launched a revolt against the Americans. The United States was at war again. About 100,000 Americans eventually fought in the Philippines. Finally, Aguinaldo was captured in 1901. The U.S. rule in the Philippines went on for decades. For better or worse, the United States had become a world power.

In 1900, many Americans had thought of the Spanish-American War as "splendid" and "little." Fourteen years later, World War I began in Europe. The United States stayed neutral for three years. Finally, Americans couldn't ignore their new role in the world. In 1917, American troops went into battle again.

There was nothing splendid or little about this next war. The fighting spread around the globe. New weapons made battle more dangerous. Some 53,000 Americans died. That's more than 100 times the number of deaths in Cuba. The United States had new **privileges** in the world. It also had new duties. The world had entered a new era.

Glossary

agency (*noun*) an action; something done to reach a goal

ambush (*verb*) to attack from a hiding place

ammunition (*noun*) bullets or cannon balls fired from a weapon

assassinate (*verb*) to murder for political reasons

brigade (*noun*) a unit of soldiers

board (*verb*) to get on a ship, plane, or train

campaign (*noun*) a series of plans used to win something

decline (*noun*) the state of getting worse or smaller

determination (*noun*) strong will to complete a task

impatient (*adjective*) restless; in a hurry

invest (*verb*) to spend money on something in the hope you will earn more money back

liberate (*verb*) to free somebody or something

linger (*verb*) to stay a while longer

Manifest Destiny (*noun*) the 19th-century belief that Americans had a duty to expand the nation throughout North America

negotiate (*verb*) to talk with someone in order to reach an agreement

overwhelmed (*adjective*) given more than one can handle

plantation (*noun*) a large farm worked by many people

privilege (*noun*) an advantage or special right

regiment (*noun*) a military unit made up of two or more large groups of soldiers

resign (*verb*) to leave a job or position

revolutionary (*noun*) a person who works to bring about change

strategy (*noun*) a plan for achieving a goal

tabloid (*noun*) a small newspaper that carries sensational stories

truce (*noun*) a temporary agreement to stop fighting

unify (*verb*) to bring together

Idioms

corner of the globe (*page 14*) any place in the world
The grand prize on the game show was a trip to any corner of the globe.

Index